reathe...
The Key To Finding Inner Peace
In A Hectic World

irdie Chesson

Miss Birdie's Books, Inc.
New York

ISBN:
978-1-732-16628-8
Copyright 2019 by Birdie Chesson

This book is dedicated to my son Bam.
Your earthly belief in me when I didn't have it
for myself saved us both. I'll be eternally
grateful for your love and trust.

Table of Contents

Page	Chapter	
5	Foreword	
8	One	Running In Place
14	Two	Dreamer
27	Three	The Jump
40	Four	Doing The Work
47	Five	Back To New York
61	Six	Ties that Bind
70	Seven	Unconditional Love
80	Eight	The Girl That Cried Mommy Wolf
91	Nine	Tuning in
111	Acknowledgments	
113	Breathe – The Processes	

FOREWORD

What a difference a year makes!

It took an entire year to change the limiting beliefs that held me back from where I wanted to be in all of the different stages of my life.

When I wrote my first memoir, Saggy Boobs, Stretch Marks and Saddle Bags, I was in the belief that I was ready to *'Rejoin My Life'* as I call it. And I did. But soon afterwards, I fell on my face again.

I was ashamed. How did I end up here again? And what was worse, now I was homeless with the glaring issues from the past that I thought I had dealt with, staring at me, taunting me. I was a hypocrite, an imposter. Helping others change their lives while I was a mess.

So, I stripped my own self bare, looked at my limiting beliefs at the core so that I could leave it all behind to have the life I always dreamed of living and giving to Bam.

It was so important for me to articulate to you what happened and bring home that it was only my own attraction that kept bringing those same things to me in different forms. It eventually saved me.

I had to look at what I was attracting and change my vibe accordingly. I learned my lessons and now I can tell you how. My hope is to help you find your own point of attraction through the clarity of my example & show that you can obtain the success that you want and deserve too.

Love and Light,
Birdie

CHAPTER ONE
Running In Place

With thunderous applause in the background as I walked off the stage, I looked to the back of the room and saw my son Bam, looking at me with the same bright look in his eyes as he did when he was happy, amazed and full of wonder.

Suddenly flooded with emotion, my eyes welled up with tears, which isn't really hard for me, but I was still so happy at that familiar look he gave me. It had been a long time coming.

There was no way that he could know how much I truly appreciated his love and support all of these years. His eyes always told the truth.

"I trust you, Mom." echoed in my ears.

It has been only months ago that he said those very words as he and I was on the discount bus going down to Tampa, Florida. It was with a whirlwind of emotions that we left New York. It was a very unpopular decision, in my small circle of family and friends. Although they didn't talk much about it, it was more like a deafening silence as they watched me 'suddenly snatch my son and leave'. Being stunned and in disbelief was where their silence came from.

The theory that I was out of my mind wasn't that I was to leave so suddenly; it also came from me telling everyone that my sudden decision to egress came suddenly through my dreams.

Yes, I said dreams. I've been having dreams all of my life but, for the first time in my life, I was finally listening to myself. I was going to go for what I wanted.

You know that *big* dream. The dream of living the best life that you can give your children.

That dream for me was giving that quality of life *outside* of living in public housing.

Bam and I were living on the affluent Upper West Side of Manhattan, across the street from Lincoln Center. I called it our great point of reference. The apartment was small and cozy, but it was ours.

We had everything at our fingertips. Living in the city that never sleeps, with tons of activities to do and being at the epicenter of *everything* and easy access to get *everywhere*. Central Park was our playground and being in Midtown was everything I ever wanted.

But it was still the projects. The pride of living in the city was always laced with a side of shame that it was public housing. Who cares if you're an entrepreneur, strong independent woman if your 2-bedroom rent in Manhattan is only $720 in the 'ghetto'? Yes, It's a great money deal but there's a stigma of public housing that you're poor and lazy, sitting on the government assistance and/or taking advantage of 'the system'.

I had friends that didn't know that I lived in public housing and that I was still struggling. I felt like an imposter.

I was set on only being in public housing until I could afford to get out. But it seemed like it would never happen. It's a system that is built to never end, generations long. I know that there are tons of people that feel the way that I do. But that's another thought for another day.

I was grateful to have my comfortable apartment that I made into a home but I was very uncomfortable with my financial circumstances.

I am an entrepreneur. I have several endeavors that stretch into different industries and would exhaust any regular person. But I had a vision.

Create the life that I'd love, be proud of and enjoy. Make money as we slept. But the truth was, that none of my businesses were making any money at all and I was struggling to keep my head above water. I worked jobs and stayed up day and night to keep my dreams alive because I refused to quit.

As I mentioned in my first memoir, the last time I quit on myself, I started having seizures.

Then years later, I had developed heart problems from stress. I loved my job working with children but the job consumed so much of my time and energy that I wasn't there for my son like I wanted to be. But we needed the money. The day that I almost went into cardiac arrest was when I knew that I had to make changes but since I didn't know how, I still stayed.

Then Bam was attacked coming home from school. He didn't even tell me right away. I had to hear it from his school.

I was totally out of balance. My parenting was suffering. My health suffered. Bam wasn't safe in our neighborhood and my business needed to be brought back to life, *again*.

Knowing the *how* I chose to be true to myself literally affected my heart and mind, and now was affecting Bam, quitting the job that I loved to do wasn't an option anymore.

I decided that I had to put my attention where it was the most important, back to being a better mom to Bam and creating a great life for us on my own terms. When I quit my job, I decided to re-examine, regroup and restart my business.

Now I can make sure that I was available at all times for my son and anything that he needed while I focused on my business. No more outside distractions that were taking me away from him. With a renewed focus, I was back to creating our 'good life'.

That's what I always thought I was doing but I still felt like I was running in place. Why wasn't I ever breaking through?

With all of the blood, sweat and tears I put into it, why was my business still stalling?

Chapter Two
Dreamer

One Friday evening, I wanted to get some how-to information for helping my business so I went to Barnes & Noble to see if there was a book that could help me.

After searching, I grabbed a batch of books and looked for somewhere to sit and quickly look through them to see if I'd buy anything that could help me.

Usually I go to the seating area but my eyes were drawn to an empty spot on the windowsill. I grabbed my basket and rolled it there and realized that my other hand was empty. The hot cup of coffee that I once held was missing.

I retraced my steps and found it but when I came back, a woman wearing all black and a humongous afro-shaped wig was now sitting in the windowsill next to where my basket was. I slowly moved my basket over and cautiously sat down on the other side.

In my peripheral, I saw that the woman is sobbing. I handed her a tissue.

"Thank you, Sis." She said quietly.

I smiled clumsily and went back to reading. She spoke up, still sobbing. "Do you know where there's a room for rent tonight?"

"No, sorry." I said, without looking up. She turned her body towards me.

She continued, "I just got here from Miami this evening and didn't really think the move through. New York is nothing like what I remember after 12 years. I thought I could find a cheap room. Now my suitcase wheel is broken and I'm dragging it around with nowhere to go."

When I looked over at her bag, it was bad, and the bottom of the bag was getting worn from where it dragged on the ground. She needed help but I was trying to stay focused on why I was there in the first place.

I said, "Well, we have to follow ourselves and realize that it always works out, even when you think it isn't. Sometimes the path takes longer to get to because we take the long way to get to it. But it still always works out."

She smiled. "Thank you for that. I just need to get through the night for now."

I became more conscious of what I received in life when I learned about the Law of Attraction and that I created my own reality. The concept of The Laws made sense in my mind but I was really new at *living* the thought process behind it.

I was always able to use my voice to talk to the world about creating in their own lives, while I was attempting to create in my own.

My concepts were of creating together with my audience and I always made it clear that we are all on this journey of co-creation.

Emphasizing that I am only human and that I'm still learning too and was what always helped ease the imposter syndrome I felt in my life. Everyday, I used my newly created positive vibes to talk and take myself out of any negative feelings that I had about my own life and share it with the world in real time.

I knew that I was only scratching the surface of my potential with my procrastination and coasting in mediocrity. I just had to get my stride and find my way.

Overall, I wasn't unhappy but I definitely wasn't happy. I was doing what we all do from time to time. Living my life without thought, just going with the flow. Not creating but steering through the hard times, just reacting to what life gave me.

So now that I was working from home full time, I could focus on creating, making that quality life for us. But after not working on myself or my business for so long, I was looking for a place to start again. That was the reason I was in this bookstore in the first place.

So seeing this woman, desperate to find her own way, I totally understood her plight. I knew that I was in a position to help, even if it was for just tonight. It was getting late and the bookstore was closing soon. I hadn't made dinner yet so I had to get home to Bam.

"You can sleep on my couch and we'll figure it out tomorrow." Her broken suitcase was so heavy that we had to take a taxi.

We dropped off her suitcase at the house and all went out to dinner. I listened to her story, giving her as much encouragement as I could. She was a nice woman but you could tell that she was afraid and lost.

Later that night, I had a vivid dream. It was a dream that told me that I had to change my living room around. It was so real, something that felt mandatory.

So the next day, I asked my friend Elijah to come over and he helped me move my living room around. He was a light worker, someone who was also trying to guide me through using rather unconventional means, but he was a great friend that I found resonance with. When you're on a journey, you pick up some friendships that you need. He definitely didn't mind this huge feat.

After he left, the woman and I decided to use the opportunity to get rid of some things.

Later that evening, Bam's father came to pick him up for the weekend. He always lingered around, which always bothered me, but this time, upon seeing the woman, he picked up Bam and quickly left.

Noticing the abruptness of Doug's behavior, the woman commented, "I'm sorry if I interrupted anything."

I was just glad that he had left without protest or small talk, that I just smiled and told her that it was fine and that she didn't interrupt anything. I went on with my night, still getting rid of things and the woman went on reading her book on the couch.

Before I went to bed, I saw a dream catcher on my front door.

It seemed like an odd place to put one but I always heard that dream catchers warded off bad dreams and spirits. It was definitely something that I knew nothing about so I didn't say anything. It was unnerving that she didn't ask me first.

The woman was nice but there was something about her that was unsettling. She had a dark energy but you could tell that she was looking for some peace. I was glad that I could give some relief to her in her situation but her vibes were definitely throwing me off.

Whenever Bam was gone, I'd camp out in the living room and concentrate on working on myself or my businesses without interruptions, but since she had come, I felt confined to the back of the house. But it was temporary so I put it out of my mind and worked in my room.

When I went to bed that night, I had another dream that told me that the woman had to leave immediately. A man told me that the woman was running from something bad and now it was following her and coming to my home.

The dream scared the daylights out of me because it was a scary dream with shadows and creepy creatures that I felt brush on my skin. I never had dreams like that before.

The woman was with me for three days now and everyday the woman went to the library to go online, looking for jobs and an apartment but to no avail.

I didn't know what to say to how to tell her that she had to go and I definitely didn't know how she would react to why she had to leave so suddenly. All I knew was that this was a weird dream that really disturbed me. But I didn't say anything to her yet.

There were times that she'd creep quietly down the hallway and her sudden presence in the doorway of my room would make me jump. Something felt wrong, her vibe and mine did not mix.

Then, I found stones and crystals in my bathroom. I'm not familiar with dream catchers, stones and crystals but I think that she knew that she also felt that she needed protection from something. I knew in my heart that my dream was right about something chasing her and that she had to go.

But I didn't tell her that night and when I went to bed later that night, I had another dark dream.

In the dream, 2 men grabbed me by my arms and physically moved me, telling me that whatever she was running from was now in my house, and I had to fight it. They told me that I couldn't even bring my son back into to the home for his safety.

I woke up confused. I was definitely experiencing more clearly and defined dreams since this woman entered my life.
People were touching me in this series of dreams, but this was the first time that I actually felt anything so physical happen to me in my dreams. Needless to say, I was beyond alarmed.

I gave her notice that she had to leave. I had explained to her my dreams and that I really wanted her to find somewhere to stay but she had to leave. She appeared to understand.

Even though these dreams were different than the past, I remembered that the last time that I had dreams, I ignored them and things started falling apart in my life.

Back then, in my procrastination, I manifested disease and destruction. I was not about to make that mistake again.

Besides that, these dreams were more vivid and violent, so real. So I instantly started packing.

That night, the woman left and I breathed a sigh of relief.

Upon clearing the living room, cleaning up, I found more stones and bent steel under the rug and the cushions. There were oils and powders embedded in my couch and a red string on the handle of my front door. I removed everything from the house, then burned some sage. I thought that the threats were over.

All I had was Google to do research but I came to the conclusion that she was trying to be a protector but it was too much for me. She never explained why she did it or what it all meant, it was just all over the place. After I cleaned up, I fell asleep.

That night, in my dream, someone screamed at me that I had to leave the house. Something bad was going to happen to Bam if he came back. This dream again? Now, I wasn't taking any chances.

Bam's weekend with his father was over; I left the next morning to bring him from his father's to my sister's house.

I was so afraid of what the series of dreams meant but also wondered if I left where would we go?

All I knew what that there was what felt like imminent danger and I couldn't control it. I just had my dreams and instincts to go on.

In retrospect, it all made sense to leave. The conscious dream of wanting more, weighing in one Bam's struggles in the neighborhood and my fears of something happening to him. When the opportunity presented itself for us to leave, I knew that I would take it. But what was the clue?

Add on the pointedness of the dreams, it only took a short mental deliberation with myself, I was definitely leaving. I continued to pack up my apartment, still unsure of what was to come.

One of the biggest parts about manifestations is that you may not be able to see "the how" you will get there; you just follow the nudge that the Universe gives you. Like an, "If you build it, they will come." so get ready to be ready kind of thing. I didn't know where we were going but I knew that I had to listen.

Chapter Three
The Jump

The next morning, I got a phone call from the mother of my godchildren, Carrie. She had relocated to Florida years before.

She says, "I had a dream about you last night. I called to ask how you were." I was stuck. So I told her about the woman and my dreams to leave my apartment. She got silent. "What's wrong?" I asked.

"In my dream, I told you that something was going to happen to you and for me to tell you to come down here to Florida." We both got silent.

"Whaaaaaat?" Then we burst into laughter. It was so surreal. We hadn't talked in so long other than the short conversations about the kids and life. It's a sisterhood. We didn't need to talk everyday but she and I both know how

we feel about each other. We're sisters.
She continued, "I was showing you into a house and you said, 'I'm so glad that I left when I did.' And we both walked around your new home."

I started to get excited. It seemed like everything was aligning for us. It was such a relief to see some kind of a path.

I was nervous because I really didn't have the money to leave, and I didn't know where to get it. But here I was, being given 'the how' I was looking for.

She and I both got excited. We finished the conversation and I finished packing our suitcases. I called Bam and told him that we were moving to Florida and he was elated. The idea of a new start made him happy.

Closing up our apartment was surreal. We knew that we had to leave soon because Bam had to start school. In Florida, school begins in

August so I took Bam to his doctor appointments and made our travel accommodations.

The biggest end that I had to wrap up was telling Bam's father Doug the plans to go. I didn't know how to tell him without him thinking that I was crazy. I knew that I couldn't tell him about the lady and my series of dreams.

So when I did tell him that we would be leaving in less than a month, of course he was angry and rightfully so.

Doug was used to our routine, so he wasn't even thinking about my reasoning. He didn't care when I reminded Doug about how the neighborhood that we lived in was getting worse and that since the violence against our son, fear had kept Bam inside of the house, afraid, robbing him from any real quality of life. I told him that Bam was ready to go. The city life that we loved so much was no longer fun for Bam.

I showed him the information of the new school in Florida, the neighborhood that we were moving to and emphasized the new quality of life was what Bam deserved.

It was so clear that it was so much better than our current reality, as much as Doug wanted us to stay, that us leaving was the best thing. We would come up with a new way for him to see Bam through FaceTime, Skype and frequent visits to New York.

He tried to convince me to stay or let Bam stay with him, but the current quality of both of our lives was the reason why staying in New York was the reason that we were leaving. Staying wasn't the best thing for either of us right now.

In hindsight, I wished that he had more time to consider the weight of my decision, but we had to go. Bam stayed with his father until we left so that they could spend time with him and his brother altogether.

We've always had our differences as far as parental responsibilities go, like other co-parenting situations go, but I had always felt that Doug wasn't as present as he should have been. His mother lived in the same neighborhood as Bam and I did, which meant that Doug was in the neighborhood almost daily. But he'd still opt-out on visiting him 'off days' and wait to see our son whenever he felt like it or when it was 'his time.'

Doug had started a new family again with another baby on the way and his inability to balance it all, now affected his relationship with Bam. Bam was suffering and becoming detached and indifferent about their relationship, which saddened me. I'd bring it to Doug's attention only to be dismissed so ultimately I'd try to stay out of it.

In the decision that I made to leave, I didn't want him to think that I was minimizing his role as Bam's dad. But now despite he had to put his own feelings aside and think of what was best for our son's future. We would have to figure out the logistics later.

Doug took my decision personally, as if I was punishing him for how he took for granted his son's physical presence, but this wasn't about him or his guilt. It was always about Bam.

We both wanted to see each other's way to no avail. We didn't talk about it anymore and he finally saw us off at the bus station.
It was sad energy but I took his seeing us off physically as him reluctantly giving us his blessing.

On the bus down to Florida, Bam was excited but was nervous. Leaving familiarity behind and moving forward to uncertainty was nerve-wracking for both of us.

When we finally got to Tampa, Carrie and my godchildren greeted us. We were all so excited. We dropped off the luggage in our part of the house and went to the school to register Bam.

The energy, the sunshine and the palm trees were breathtaking. We settled in and went to the pool, as school was to start in only 2 days, to Bam's dismay.

Life in Florida was easy. Bam went to school and when he came in, he was able to go outside to play. We settled into a routine. I started looking for jobs and continued to work on my business. The jobs that I was looking for were jobs that I was used to, with children and in schools.

A few days later, we were served custody papers. Doug was suing for full custody of Bam. Bam saw the mail and crawled into a ball on the couch.

"Dad didn't give me a chance, Mom." was all that Bam kept saying.

I was sad and angry. Why couldn't Doug see that Bam's quality of life is what was for the best? Why couldn't he think about Bam right now?

Bam retreated. It was like he couldn't get happy. He felt like his father was pulling him back because he wasn't happy for him and now he didn't even want to talk to his father whenever he called.

This made the situation worse.

The papers said that I had to report to court within 2 weeks and was grateful that I was able to go to the courthouse in Florida because coming back to New York so soon was impossible.

The court date was a circus. I testified to the judge about finally having the quality of life that our son deserved.

The judge agreed that it was a better quality of life but was upset that I left before cementing a feasible custody agreement with Doug.
I agreed with her and apologized and told her what Bam wanted. Doug told the judge that he wanted the judge to force us back, even if it meant my refusal to result in jail.

So where were we going to go if we had to come back? I had already packed the apartment up. Going back wasn't an option.

Bam and I both were upset but we tried not to let it dominate our thoughts but it was hard because the toxic energy of the custody battle permeated the vibe of being in Florida.

Carrie and the kids were great. The biggest issue in the house was the abuse that Carrie was going through at the hands of her boyfriend. I felt so defenseless to help her.

They were in the process of breaking up because of their constant conflicts before we even came down to Florida. So when we arrived in Tampa, I was under the impression that he was leaving or had left. But he was still there, his energy dominated the overall house but me and Bam had the solace of our own part of the house. We had a generous space.

He said that he decided to stay to get himself in a better financial footing before he finally left her. It was grueling to say the least. It was like watching a knife going through her heart, being covered by a band-aid only to be knifed slowly again… and again.

It would've been ideal if the situation between them was more stable and abuse wasn't such an easy thing to revert to for him.

It was such a toxic situation in the house that what mental escape from the thoughts of the custody battle in New York was magnified by the constant fighting and toxic energy. Peace was definitely hard to find.
Her children seemed numbed by the long-term violence. Carrie endured because she had a high profile job with the state and because of my custody situation, I couldn't call the police when things got bad. I couldn't give Doug the ammunition to take Bam. Carrie and I were both trapped.

Taking walks at sundown was what the children and I started looking forward to. We'd laugh and talk about our day, take pictures of the sunsets and talk. Then everyone would take baths and go to bed.

Overall, in the house, when it was great, it was great. But soon the toxicity of their relationship spilled over into my son and I's presence in the house.

Now he made it seem that it was **us** being in the house that was the couple's problem. It became the reason for him to be set off at her.

Carrie and I knew that it wasn't the truth but she was between a rock and a hard place. I felt so sorry for her but all I could do was help support her by giving positive words of encouragement, helping with the children and helping by buying groceries and cooking.

As the conflicts with her boyfriend reached a fever pitch, I went inward.

At night, I started doing processes. Focus wheels and writing positives to the situation. I was working on how I'd feel once Bam and I had our own home.

The biggest problem for me was, because the financial burden was on Carrie, I felt that helping her financially with all of what little I had, I couldn't save any money.

The processes, vision boards and focus wheels I did were useless because everything I had to do and was dealing with contradicted the energy.

I had locked down the apartment when I left, now my neighbor called and told me that I had an eviction notice on my door. In all of the commotion, I never turned in the keys or completely cleaned out the apartment. In the months that I had left NY, I stopped paying rent. I had no money to spread around. I was living hand to foot in Florida.

I borrowed money from a family member and Bam and I went back to New York. I cleaned out the apartment, put our essentials into the storage space that my mother had and Bam got to spend time with his brother and their father.

Although I wanted to cut ties, I hadn't completely left New York behind. There were still belongings I left that I thought that I would be able to retrieve when I had our own space but I was spread too thin.

So I decided to make keys of the apartment and give away the things that I couldn't take with me or put into storage.

As I boxed up the things I was keeping, (memories and Bam's baby pictures) I was reminded that within the Laws of Prosperity and Abundance (circulation and reciprocity) whatever you give with a blessing and good intentions, makes room for equal or better.

Learning that and following the Tao Te Ching with Wayne Dyer, made me see that I had put feelings into objects and perhaps that was keeping us tied to New York.

The neighbors and friends got my favorite chair, TV's, beds, dressers, a lot of clothes, pots and pans and a lot of other nice treasures that Bam and I had picked up along the way. I had left so much behind for them that they thought something was wrong with me.

But I wanted them to have the blessing, letting it all go became easier. I wasn't losing anything. I was gaining a new future. Although I'd miss them, they were only things.
 Even though that thought was the primary consensus, the 'lack' part of me still I felt like now I lost everything.

By the end of the weekend, I had finally dropped off the keys and said goodbye to the apartment again, leaving New York behind and returned to Florida at Carries' house.

Chapter Four
Doing the Work

One the bus back to Florida, my mind was racing. I had to search for answers somewhere. We were now at the point of no return. What was I supposed to learn from all of this?

That's the question, right? They always say not to feel sorry for yourself, but to look for the lesson within.

To tell you the truth, at the time I didn't know what the lesson was supposed to be. All I did know was that I was saying goodbye left and right, giving things away, fighting for custody again.

Now I was going back to Carrie's immersed in the house drama and no steady income to leave. Florida was our home now and I had to make it work.

My vibe was all over the place. No one was doing this to me. I was attracting all of this. I knew that no matter how positive I tried to be, I couldn't change the vibe in the house. I also couldn't ignore the turmoil in my own life. So I tried to be invisible.

Since the only time I could have peace was when I left the house, taking walks was my saving grace. Now I was out all day, listening to books and sitting to meditate. I did dream maps and affirmations, looking for peace from somewhere. Coming inside to work and help Carrie care for the kids and cooking was my routine.

Even though I bought groceries, Carrie's boyfriend was complaining about me eating so I started fasting and did more meditating. I was finally bulletproof to me but Bam was still sliding into depression. The toxicity and the custody stuff were really getting to him.

So I was taking him with me on walks and he found peace in the pool, so he'd swim all day when he could. We just needed to stay positive.

Because I wasn't getting work in Florida, I was using my time working on my business. I tried to finish the writing projects that I had started but couldn't find the words.

I had gotten a few editing jobs and made a few notebooks and planners and even started an online store with products I created for sale to help make money.

But there was this shame that I felt that the financial burden fell on Carrie and it didn't help that her boyfriend was very vocal about it, although he wasn't contributing to the household. He was saving for his own egress.

The only perspective that I had was that it was a "he" issue and not a 'me issue. Misery loves company and I wasn't joining it. It made him angry that I was untouchable except through making Carrie pay for it.

The clarification gave me a small relief but it didn't change the conversation or the vibe. Carrie was trapped by his spiteful anger and the uncertainty that hosting us had brought.

I didn't know that getting a job and our own place was going to be so hard. I couldn't even save money, I only made enough to buy groceries and pay my bills and for essentials.

To make matters worse, I was running out of medication for my seizures and couldn't qualify for health insurance in Florida. It was getting bad and I felt like I couldn't catch a break. But I tried to stay positive that things would turn around.

I made friends that made the hard times easier. Friends that showed me that Florida was definitely a great choice. But I'd come back to Carrie's house, back to the issues I was trying to avoid. I really wanted to make a nice paycheck and leave Carrie's house for our own place.

To keep our eyes on the prize, Bam and I went to open house tours to get an idea of the type of houses we'd like, get positive visuals of what we wanted to work towards. Even the amenities we wanted to enjoy were on our vision board.

We knew that we wanted to stay in the neighborhood and Bam liked his school and Florida was strict about school zones, if we moved out of the area, Bam would have to change schools.

Another court date almost resolved the custody situation but at the end the proceedings went left when Doug asked for a lawyer.

He was highlighting my instability and wanted to know my income. The thought made me panic because the truth was that I subconsciously, even I felt that I *was* unstable. I didn't want to own that I actually felt that way. But I had to deal with that reality.

There were the bogus belief systems I conditioned myself into from the past rearing its ugly head and now it was magnified. I was attracting more problems from the thought activation. When you focus on something, it makes it more. Carrie's boyfriend's attacks emphasized it and now in Doug's need for transparency I felt exposed. But still not one solution in sight. It was time for some kind of change.

After having a seizure and a heated exchange with Carrie's boyfriend, I knew that I had to leave Carrie's house ASAP. It was glaringly clear that we weren't ready for Florida.

Before we left, our friends in Florida even offered to give us shelter, but somewhere to live wasn't our only problem. I couldn't get more medicine, couldn't get health insurance. Then I got notification from Bam's lawyer that for the next court date, that we'd get a new judge for our case.

I felt like the judge needed to see me and Bam needed to see his lawyer. I decided that I should come back to New York for the court date.

I knew that I had to regroup and figure out a plan in New York to go back on our own terms for our own home and a consistent livelihood. I didn't want a repeat of events. Remember, wherever you go, you take yourself with you.

Christmas time was fast approaching and one of my great friends Polly gifted us two one-way plane tickets back to New York.

I resolved to come back to where my heart settled on, a home in Florida. But I wasn't sure when we'd be able to come back so I put our things in storage and 2 days before Christmas, we came back to New York.

Chapter Five
Back to NY

Flying back to NY, there was a deafening silence between Bam and me. Neither one of us were happy to come back. But I wanted to end this war with his father and after what was going on in Carrie's house and my health, I just needed piece of mind.

The holidays came and went. I wanted to see what money I could make in New York but didn't plan to stay long, so I applied for homeschooling for Bam in Florida. He was approved, for a full year so we started.

With no money to come back to Florida to a new place, we dug in our heels and just braved the New York winter cold, physically and figuratively.

Doug and I went to court and the judge saw how agreeable I was and saw that I acted in Bam's best interests.

I was able to retain full & sole custody with a new visitation agreement in place and he dropped the suit. We got permission to live in Florida. But unbeknownst to him, he had already got what he wanted. We were back in NYC.

I had even heard that things with Carrie and her boyfriend had got even worse. I could only be there for Carrie with well wishes because now Bam and I had more of our own issues to deal with.

So I went back to working on my business in my mother's living room and taught Bam during the day. Time flew and we slid into a never-ending routine that drained us.

Bam kept asking when were we leaving to go back to Florida and I had no answers for him. I was still working hard on making money so we could get off of my mother's couch.

But I understood his frustration. He was a teenage boy that needed his own space. He always had it and he definitely deserved it. He was ripped away from the sunshine, great neighborhood and a school he was fond of.

Now that we were back in New York, we were right back where we started. Only this time, on top of everything, Bam and I didn't even have our own home anymore.

We didn't have our belongings, not even a bed. We just had the clothes and essentials that we traveled with.

I tried to give Bam the perspective of what we did have: my mother's warm apartment and couch and most of all, we still had each other and our health.

But who was I fooling? Some days it was hard for me to stay consistently positive. I was really trying to keep the smiles and the encouragement and perspective of what I knew about creating my own reality. I could spout the words but my vibration was definitely lacking.

I was talking to a teenage boy. Although that perspective of appreciation helped me thrive and survive, the rationale fell on deaf ears for Bam. Bam just wanted what he deserved, what I promised him: quality of life.

I was still homeschooling Bam so I just continued his instruction so that he could stay on track. His father and I were finally done with court and I was relieved with that part but I was so unsettled in my spirit about it.

I was free of this portion of the drama between us but I knew that there was something else I needed to settle with us.

I was definitely bitter. We had gone through this before. It seemed like every time he didn't get his way, he'd haul me to court. This past time was our third foray into New York's Family Court system.

Our relationship was always complicated. I knew that there were unresolved issues between us that spilled into bitter fights. We were always able to get along because we genuinely care about each other and love our son but there was an unspoken anger between us that affected how we co-parent and communicate.

It seemed that I would try to be accommodating but every time I'd give an inch, he would take a mile and it was exhausting. It was like a game of mercy at times. What was his hold on me?

Although me and Bam loved it, things weren't easy in Florida and now that we were forced back to New York through so many circumstances, that it couldn't have just been a coincidence.

Not being able to get health insurance or get a job or drum up enough business to get our own place. Then that my friend was going through abuse that made it unbearable to stay in the house made it all abundantly clear that although we felt at home in Florida, Florida wasn't ready for us yet.

What did I learn about our extended visit? Well, when you leave things behind, you still take **you** with you.

Then my thoughts were: Was I running? What was I running to? Why was I avoiding what I was supposed to be doing? What was I supposed to do?

Then I remembered where my mind was before I decided to go. I was supposed to focus on business. Rebuilding the foundation of my business.

I was being taken off track so much, so easily, so when was I going to finally do what I was meant to do? To be honest with myself, I was so unsettled in Florida, just like I was in New York only months before.

I was looking for a job in Florida when I was supposed to finish books and market myself, just like when I was in New York.

When you're supposed to go in one direction, the path won't open up in the other. The universe is funny that way.

I know that I was supposed to leave my Project apartment behind because the law of places says that when you are supposed to move, the universe will make your circumstances and surroundings so unbearable that you will have no choice but to choose. We attracted that with Bam's attack, my growing imposter's syndrome and the crazy dreams from during the lady's visit.

The law of prosperity says that in order to get better, you have to leave the former things behind.

Well, check and check.
I gave up what I was uncomfortably comfortable with... twice. But what else was I supposed to do?

Coming back to New York, I felt like a failure.

I had originally left because I just wanted to win. I felt so much more loss than gain. I even wallowed for a minute before I caught myself. I didn't want to attract more sad and bad either.

Upon coming back, all of the friends and family that didn't want us to leave in the first place were happy to see us back.

I told everyone that our stay was temporary, just to regroup in order to jump back to Florida.

Friends wanted us to pick up and resume the fun and games and back to the life that we had in New York. But I didn't answer or go. I was different. I wanted to be laser focused on being where we were supposed to be.

 A lot of people grew angry that I didn't want to participate in the festivities and didn't understand my distance. I was going through a spiritual awakening like I never felt before. I was so different inside and I couldn't explain it.

I was rediscovering myself in all of the things that I immersed myself in, the journey that I had started when I was in Florida.

I was also traumatized from all of the experiences that I attracted, in survival mode for so long, with no answers of how I was going to make it happen. I needed peace and clarity. Once I found that, I could see ourselves clear and change our lives.

All I knew that was what I didn't want. Step one of the creative process… Asking for the improvement.

I had to be ok with that fact that this was no one else's journey but mine. It wasn't for anyone else to understand. I couldn't care if anyone else thought I was nuts. I had to keep going.

I started to detach from people even more. I didn't want anyone's advice or words, I just had to get in alignment with myself.

I stopped thinking. Sounds funny but the Law of Attraction goes by vibes and emotions, the way you feel. I didn't want to keep the way that I felt about myself and the journey alive. Those things definitely overwhelmed how I felt.

As someone who always thinks, it was hard. I had to take my time. I had to learn to breathe again. Stop my thoughts by focusing on my breathing.

I started taking walks again to clear my mind. I started looking at the sky for clouds that looked like fire and birds in the sky like they did in Florida.

Back there, the more stressed I was, the more I redirected my thoughts towards peace and found it. I was centered and focused. It didn't matter that Carrie's boyfriend didn't appreciate it. Maintaining my vibration was more important.

I didn't realize that I was being planted, broken down to my foundation to start over with the right bricks and cement. I was to be built to last and succeed. This time was going to be different and I was never to have to ever look back again.

So, what did I want?

1) A successful business and many streams of income that I'd be able to secure me and my son's future and make money while we slept.

2) A home for my son and I to enjoy.

3) A great co-parenting relationship with his father.

4) A million+ dollars wouldn't hurt.

How was I going to manifest that?
The Laws suggest that by knowing that I deserved it all, not bits and pieces of what I wanted but ALL OF IT. All I had to do was tune in and allow the result of all of my seeding, sowing and planting period and allow the Universe to show me my path to it all.

My life circumstances already begged for the answer. Funny thing about answers, they're always there. When you ask a question, even if you don't know the answer, the answer is somewhere. I just didn't know where to find it. None of us really do.

But the question and the answer is never in the same frequency.

So as hands-on as we people tend to be, we have to realize that it's the Universe, Inner Self, God or whomever or whatever you believe in that brings that to you.

Bare bones: All I knew was what I wanted and why. That was it.

Time is never what we think. We're so much in a hurry to make things happen that we mess it up. How and when we get there is none of our business.

It's like fast moving traffic, do u just drive into it? No! You yield to traffic, waiting for an opening and *then* go with the flow.

Now all I needed was to find my opening and go with the flow.

It kind of reminded me of the Serenity Prayer: "Grant me the serenity to accept the things I cannot change, the courage to change the things I can and the wisdom to know the difference."

It's applicable to <u>everyone</u> in <u>every</u> situation.

That meant that I could only focus on what I could control and had to let the rest go. At this point all I had was, my health, my mind, my hands, my son and my independence.

What was I blessed with? My mom's home and patience and best of all, my son's love and trust.

Most of all, I had to be at peace with the rest of it. Satisfied with my mom's couch, homeschooling my son with limited resources and no real income besides occasional payments from past jobs and grateful for child support from my son's father.

I went to the state and got temporary food stamps to help my mother and got health insurance for me and Bam.

I was literally back to square one. But you know what? This time I was not ashamed or apologetic. I was confident that in my stripped down state and through my alignment, I was going to find everything I needed.

What inner work did I have to do? What was in the foundation that I was to build up so that we were indestructible? Why did we seem to end up in the same place but now at the lowest point?

What was it?

Chapter Six
The Ties That Bind

Shame. It was always shame. Shame had followed me from when I failed at my business. When we lived in Public Housing. When I had gotten homeless. When I needed food stamps and government medical. I was ashamed.

By *staying* ashamed, I reacting to whatever was thrown at me instead of using my inner power to create a way and sit from a seat of strength. Imagine the vibe from shame. You can't get anywhere or anything from there.

Whenever Doug took me to court, I could never talk about how I was truly supporting us. Money came so sporadically that learning how to save & stretch a dollar, child support and the fact that I could walk everywhere I needed to go helped.

I was ashamed now and didn't want people to know that we were truly struggling as bad as we were. People didn't even know that we had come back.

I had reached a point that I couldn't even do my encouraging videos anymore. I felt like a fraud. I knew what to say to help others but I was stuck on how to help myself. I only spoke through the clarity of my example and I was not clear anymore.

Even when I started writing this book, when it was time for me to even be honest in my writing or express how I felt, I was ashamed. I was good at deflecting and giving good advice but I was ashamed of my own life.

Limiting beliefs will hold you back every time. And if you don't learn from it, the lesson will keep presenting itself in the most damaging ways. I can attest to that.

Knowing my intent was for Bam and I to go back to Florida once the custody was settled, I needed a better plan for us to not just survive,

but for us to prosper.
In order to face it, I had to get honest.

I needed to find my own source connection. I knew what I had to do. First order of business, drop the shame. Rebuild the foundation. Rejoin my own life for real.

I started with business shame. I am a serial entrepreneur. The businesses that I own and run now range from writing books and songs, to manufacturing mixed cocktails. From coaching and speaking, to designing products in our own online store.

But where was the money? I was running in place with nothing to show for it. I was still making announcements about accomplishments I had like a small child that shows off ugly art. No one was buying into me, my stuff and I was disappointed.

Those were my issues and no one else's. That lack mentality was what I was projecting so why would anyone buy into me?

I even thought at one point that no one was supporting me. But wasn't true. There were those that did encourage me and put out the good word on the things that I did.

There were people who had said out of their mouths that they didn't understand what I was doing so they literally wouldn't support me.

That's when I learned to keep my thoughts and ideas quiet until they were full formed and executed or I was just adding to the noise. No one was buying it anyway so what was the loss?

No one was supposed to believe in me. That was my job to believe in myself.

I had stopped believing in me and now I had to start believing in order to show Bam how to succeed.

At first I was hurt but then I thought, '*they don't owe you anything*. Just keep pushing Birdie. Just keep pushing.'

Being all the way honest about my work, there were things that I was breaking my neck to avoid. Writing projects from the past that were outlined and waiting for attention. Some of it was writers block but it was also procrastination on my part. A lot of self-sabotage, self-imposed distractions and fears. I was afraid that no one would like what I had to say. Still caring about what people thought.

How about that? Me. I thought that I was fearless. Now I had to be truthful. Limiting beliefs again. Never mind if I flopped. What if I was truly great?

Hell, I knew I was great. No one else knew because all of my words were still locked in the vault of my mind.

On one hand, you shouldn't force yourself to do things that take so much energy to do. That would be "efforting". It won't come out right forced, so I had to give myself permission to wait to the right time, right?

I had to tell myself that no matter how desperate I was to start that there was a right time. At this point, I wanted *now* to be the right time, but it wasn't.

I was rebuilding my business foundation all over again. I wanted to be able to make multiple streams of income. Multiple.

There were so many other things to do in divine order. My mind has a queue so things pile up and I get overwhelmed. I've learned that when the time is right, you'll get an impulse to act. With the influx of new ideas, the queue was building up but this time I was finally getting things done because the nudges from the universe were there and I was following them, without the overwhelming feeling of not getting the other things done.

The nudges are the universe making sure you follow the path being made to what it is that you want, even if it doesn't make sense at the time.

I was now listening to myself again and walking the path, allowing my answers. Getting back to basics. Working on my businesses the way that I needed to.

I was meditating regularly. I restarted recording inspirational videos. I was writing all of my thoughts down. My mind started blossoming.

Whenever I had a dream about another project, I did it, even if it meant me stopping what I was doing at the time to make it happen. I'd finish the task and when I went back to finish the task that I stopped, it made so much more sense. I began doing things better. Listening to myself, I was working smarter, not harder.

I knew that I had to shake this manifestation of negative situations off of me if Bam and I were going to go far.

Bam was losing patience with me because while I was living in the delusion that our New York visit would be short. Meanwhile, the current reality was that we were still sequestered in the small living room at my mother's house without money or prospects of a social life.

Bam is a very social child. So when he tried to hook up with his friends from just a few months ago, he found that they had scattered and moved on. I felt so bad for him that it just started to get worse. He sunk into a sadness like the one in Florida from his father custody situation. Seeing him hurt was hard to watch. The energy that permeated the apartment was that we were all stuck. No one was happy.

What can you do but to focus on what you can change. So we focused on creating products and Bam's EDG Animations in between school and my writing. Before we knew it, summer was approaching and Bam was supposed to be with his father for the month we settled on in the agreement.

I was on a roll. As I wrote and created, the more I started to shed my layers.

I had the impulse to finish writing four books that I had started and lie sitting abandoned for years.

My thought processes were changing.
My belief systems were shifting. I always understood that I created my own reality and that nothing was happening to me, that I was actually creating and attracting the messes I was in.

Now it was so much more real to me.

So what do you do with beliefs that don't serve you? Give yourself permission to believe something else.

Chapter Seven
Unconditional Love

I finally found a stride in my work schedule that balanced with Bam's homeschooling and I was on a roll. Time flew.

We hit the summer and now Bam and I were at the precipice of the visitation agreement. The month of July was all Doug's. Bam was still upset with his father's imposition but understood that it was what we agreed on.

When we move back to Florida that his father's time would be limited to holidays and visits. I only emphasized that his father loved him and wanted much needed quality time with him.

The day that his father was supposed to pick him up, he calls me to cancel.

"I'm not going to be able to take him this month."

Silence. I was infuriated. But I kept my cool.

"Why? You know what? It doesn't matter. Do you know what you put me through for this? For July?"

"Well, we've put each other through things."

I was trying to contain myself. "Ok. Talk to you later." I hung up.

I started crying. Uncontrollably crying. My mother closed the door and let me cry in silence no one could hear me from the bedroom.

The prime reason and dark cloud over our lives in Florida was to give this matter of custody and visitation our full attention and this is what happens when we get to the time you're supposed to have?

A huge portion of the negative energy that kept snowballing was due to the horrible feelings about myself in taking care of Bam.

Worthlessness, instability, you name it, I felt it. I exuded the shame that a custody matter implies to a mother. Not to mention the hurt Bam went through. So much negativity stemmed from what ensued thereafter. Bam and I had to start over, sleeping on my mother's couch with makeshift workstations and broken promises, keeping up our son and I's morale; trying to stay positive, saying to him and myself that this situation was only temporary and this is what is what this comes to?

In that moment, I was so lost. I couldn't stop crying. I buried my face in the pillows and cried out loud. I couldn't control how hard I cried.

I was mostly upset with myself because how I allowed myself to me moved by this man's whims was now up front and center.

I needed to cry. I got it out. Ten minutes later, I got a phone call from his other son's mother, Arlene. She heard the tears still stuck in my throat when I said, "Hello."
"Hey Girl. He told me what was up. How about I take the boys this week since you had them last week and we figure it out."

Her voice was always soothing. We had formed a bond because our sons are brothers and it is so important for them to stay close together, no matter what ever transpired before and during our children's upbringing with their father.

I breathed a sigh of relief. "That sounds good." It felt good that she understood what I went through with our children's father but I also knew that I still had to work through my own issues with him.

The hold that he had on me that made me bend over backwards to whatever he requested. How when he'd take the boys for the weekend, he'd camp out in my living room with the boys and wouldn't leave.

Those weekends weren't relief for me, it was an odd settlement that I didn't want, that dysfunction that he was able to move on but I was stuck within.

In that moment of overwhelming tears I realized that I owed him absolutely nothing. That he felt entitled to take advantage of my freedom and kindnesses and that when I took Bam out of the state that he felt like I ripped the way of life that he was used to away from him. He took it personally.

From the time that we split several years ago, all I wanted was for him to spend time with our son. I wanted that when he moved on that he didn't forget our child. So I always made it easy for him.

All he wanted was for me to continue to make it easy for him to come in and out of our lives.

No more.

I was getting off of the wild train ride. No more easy access into my life.

We hadn't been together for over ten years and he was still dictating how I lived.

There was a freedom in this clarity. For the longest time, I felt freedom from him when I dried my tears.

From now on, he was only going to get what he was entitled to. No more access to me. Only give him access to our son. I wasn't going to try to cultivate a friendship with him, because when I did, he only felt entitled to be in my life. I don't even think that he knew that that was what he was doing. He just wanted things the way that he was used to them being.

Now what?
Since our son is still a minor, there is the matter of making plans for him. But that was it. Just strictly plans for co-parenting.

How was I going to change the bitterness that I felt?

Since everything is attraction, I had to realize that he wasn't asserting himself into my existence.

That he wasn't the one that really controlled my life. I attracted this relationship.

It was me. All me. To change it, I had to change me. Here was the ask: How did I want to *feel* about my son's father?

I wanted to appreciate that he loved our son. I wanted to feel like he was a good father.

So I decided that that's what I would focus on. How I wanted my relationship with him to be. To not over-empathize or be understanding of whatever was going on in his personal life to bend over backwards to make life easier for him. I was definitely no longer giving him access to my life.

If he couldn't fulfill his obligations to his son as his father, that life would go on. No more of me enabling him and his behavior. I wish I had come to this realization sooner but here we were. Better late than never.

I also wanted to give our son the power to say how he felt about events instead of me being the voice of reason, to mind my own business. His relationship with his father was no longer my business. No more niceties, I would abide by the agreements and keep our relationship above board.

I took my feelings about him and I and walked away with clean hands, knowing that I did my part and that I would no longer compensate or overcompensate for what I thought our son needed. Step back so that there was true transparency. I wish him the best and walk away.

All of the sequence of events that kept happening between us brought me to this point. Right here, right now.

I thought of the times that I bought tickets to events that created memories for him and his sons. I always took pictures to cement those memories so that our son would have them. Called him to make him accountable for things that should have come natural to him.

I was trying to make him be the father that he didn't have growing up and that father that he promised me that he'd be when I gave birth. But who was doing that work? Me. I was exerting myself into his experience as a father. So when I moved to Florida, how dare I take it away!

Even if he felt justified, I still felt attacked and vice versa. But I also had to realize that even this was attraction.

Why was I attracting this? I didn't know the answer to that yet. But I definitely had to figure my end out before the situation repeated itself yet again. How was I going to stop this? I had to stop letting my feelings about what I thought a father-son relationship that he didn't work for, consume how I lived my own life.

I let it all go. Now it was his turn and he was going to have to do his own work.

To have unconditional love for someone, you have to allow it. You can't let the circumstances around you dictate the terms. You keep creating yourself in the relationship and naturally and let things happen, while staying the person you want to be. Not fight it but allow it to progress.

I had to allow a relationship that was positive with this man or not have one at all.
We could not even be friends because we didn't have healthy boundaries yet. He felt entitled to my life and because of that hold, Bam and me were getting nowhere.

I was reacting to him before, not consciously creating. So within cultivating this new relationship, I would limit our interactions, be positive when we did have to have them and I would allow what kind of co-parenting vibes that I wanted to create to evolve. No more, no less.

That was how I had to deal with people around me now. Create the relationships that I wanted to have through my own behavior and expectations and not assert myself to change things. Just change myself. The relationships had no choice but to evolve and adjust according to what I put out.
No more exertion.

Chapter Eight
The Girl that Cried Mommy Wolf

I had started my motivational speaking practice only a year before, starting with my videos on social media after I left my job (the one that almost gave me a heart attack.) I was getting introspective then and was looking for answers.

I had come across Lisa Nichols and her story was so similar to mine when she had reached her lowest point and I was now in mine. I started speaking my truth and through my own transparency, I was finding my answers.

I still didn't learn all of my lessons: I still wasn't listening to myself all of my life from the first time my inner being spoke to me. The only difference now was that I was over 20 years older now.

The echoes of *"Do the right thing."* was always haunting me.

When I was 17, I didn't leave and go to college. I didn't listen to my impulse to go. Despite getting a scholarship, I stayed to take care of my mother, doing what she wanted me to do, *the right thing*. I started having seizures.

When I was 27, I didn't leave my son's father because I wanted to keep our family together, *the right thing.* I ignored the stomach pains I got from the stress and began exhibiting symptoms of irritable bowel syndrome.

And then at age 39, having heart issues doing a job when I should've been focused on my own business. It took being carted off to surgery to realize that was literally killing myself by not listening to *myself*.

Duh.

What else was I manifesting? Well, I have a son looking at me and suffering for *"the right thing"*, which always meant putting how I felt and how I lived in the background while helping others.
What was the "right thing"?

I did know that the wrong thing was ignoring the path that was continually unfolding towards everything that I've ever wanted. Subconsciously I was using everything around me to not go. I was doing the right thing, right?

Maybe so that if I failed, it wouldn't be my own fault, it would be because I put other's first, a noble feat. Like a martyr.

My heart knew that all I wanted was to be happy, abundance and prosperity. I wanted freedom. I wanted my son to be happy. That's all I knew. But I didn't know how I was going to get there. This was the first time I truly thought about us.

I'll never forget that day that I got a call from my son's teacher. She was stating how concerned he was about him and he had told her something disturbing.

She wouldn't tell me over the phone. I showed up the next day and she told me that my son was attacked when he got off the bus one afternoon.

I glanced over at my son, who had his head down. "Why didn't you tell me?" I didn't know that he felt that I was dismissive on my hard days and he didn't know what to do. I was ashamed. I always prided myself on having a great relationship with my son with an open floor and honesty.

We have these warped sensibilities. "Kids belong in school." "You need to listen to the teacher and staff no matter what." "Good grades are what matters." "Oh, it can't be that bad, you should have seen what I went through as a kid. You kids have it easy."

I cringe now that I think back to that time. Truth I had to face was that I wasn't there for Bam like I should've been.

My son told me through his tears, that he was in survival mode in school. He was begging me to homeschool him.
I didn't realize that at the time, bullies in school and in the neighborhood we lived in were terrorizing him.

Here I was still "doing the right thing", providing for Bam while working in a school, but I was looking out for other people's kids and not paying attention to what was actually happening to my own.

I dismissed his feelings because I was conditioned to think that that was the only way to raise a child. Especially after being a single mother for such a long time.

After years on our own, Bam's father was coming around more often than every other weekend but I needed him to still check in with Bam's mental wellness. It's so much easier to blame what someone else is not doing when you're used to it all being up to you. I was making excuses again. I was slacking with my own lack of attention and looking at what Doug didn't do to justify what wasn't getting taken care of. Bam was suffering.

Now sitting in my mother's living room at 5am every morning, either working on my businesses or preparing lessons for Bam's schooling, I'd look over at Bam sleeping on the couch and feel like I had disappointed him.

Here I am again. Shame. Feeling like I can't take care of my son. Feeling unworthy. Hiding from what I am the most ashamed of. Not having enough. Not being enough.

Wait. WHAT?

How could I even think that way? Every decision that I ever made was for the benefit of my Bam. He knew it. Deep down and sometimes overtly, I knew it. I always tried and always did my best as Bam's mother, even what I was lost and at my worst.

But I was also doing us both a huge injustice by not living my absolute best life. I was holding us back because of stage fright, imposter syndrome, who do I think I was? All a big ball of mess.

I deserved blessings. He deserved to be blessed too. I didn't want any more hardships. That look of his face when we took our oversized and heavy luggage from the flight back from Florida to New York, he said, "I don't want to struggle like this anymore."

Being the best mom I could be also involved being aware and in tuned with his needs. When he told me that he felt like he was in the survival mode, I understood what that meant. It also meant I had to listen and let him know how important his voice was, that I heard it and could help him deliberately create his experience too.

Homeschooling is hard but I am his advocate, I am his first teacher and for him to have a quality life. Life lessons also included me helping him create his own reality. We don't only live our own lives by default. We also parent by default.

A roof, 3 square meals, clothing and education – bare minimum, what our legal obligations are. But do we give quality of life?

Quality clothes well made that can last, quality food that nourishes them, expanding their nutrition. A nice roof from the cold and cover when it rains but also comfort and love in the home but yet education and potentially hostile environment is in someone else's hands with no say so?

Our children are at the mercy of educational institutions and they have the power to give them tools for life or useless, outdated scenarios that they'll never use.

My son vocalized it. I had to listen, especially after his violent attack. I didn't want to lose my son physically, but I also had to think about losing him emotionally and mentally.

Homeschooling is not an option for everyone, it

is a lot of work and scheduling it is the only way that I can do it as I run our lives and businesses but it's worth it. I monitor firsthand the quality of his education. It's tailored fit to him and his educational needs.

Bam enjoys it for the most part but I was lacking in the social aspect. We were both lonely. People around us didn't understand the homeschool concept. Bam was lonely during the long days. Finding partners, foundations, mentors and programs are essential for balance. Joining a healthy community of like minds in the same homeschooling community helped us tremendously.

Finally it came together. The past didn't matter anymore; the unfruitful past beliefs didn't matter anymore. I had started to believe new things, those beliefs birthed new desires and thoughts. Then those thoughts became things. Things that I actually wanted for us.

So I couldn't curse the past, I didn't want to feel bad or ashamed about the past.

'The now' events the residuals of the past. None of what we were going through now was relevant to mine and Bam's future if I took the steps now to vibrate higher.

In my coaching practice, I always say that you have the permission to change at anytime. No situation or past belief has any bearing on how you live your future life. YOU define what that will be. And it was so important for me to teach my son that his future was within his own control.

Empowering others means nothing if you don't believe in yourself and it meant nothing if I couldn't teach my own son to do the same.

If I was going to show him his own power and that he creates his experience, I had to lead with love. Leading with love is bigger than just taking the high road. It includes looking at people and circumstances and seeing that everything always works out and that knowing that you have more power than you realize.

My job was not to just to be the best me but teach thru the clarity of my example. I had to show and prove. Becoming a respire coach meant to me that teaching others to breathe expands their mental energy by helping them quiet their minds, being conscious of their thoughts. If the momentum, was negative, to use their breathing to stop those thoughts, create new thoughts and subsequently change their lives.

I promised Bam that we wouldn't struggle anymore and I meant that promise. Now the real work had to be done on myself.

Now that I had finally gotten down to the bottom of what I felt about myself, I had to forgive myself from the mommy guilt and resolve to do better. How was I going to do that?

I'm going to feel my way through. Not get sucked into what happened in the past. The past is truly the past.

Chapter Nine
Tuning In

This book was so hard to write because I didn't want to rehash the past anymore. I was past the feelings that came with what happened. LOA makes bigger the thoughts you're thinking about. What you think about, whether you want it or not. That's the way it goes.

When I started to tell my story I wanted to pre-pave, or foretell the future that I saw. But I was also knee-deep in the "is-ness" of the hardship. So it took longer than I wanted it to write it.

Sometimes we know and understand the concept of the Laws of Attraction, but we lose our own connection because as Abraham Hicks says through Esther, "One you achieve your vibration, it's not like a college degree, it is not yours forevermore, you have to keep at it."

I had to only write about what I could that I could easily deal with because I had taken my feelings out of it. Pre-paving is like segment intending, focus wheels and vision boards. It's you telling things that you want to happen.

If you can't take how you feel out of it now, it's no good. It would be like having a dream that you don't believe. How can you expect it to come true?

I thought about when I was feeling at my lowest in Florida. Meditation saved my sanity when I needed inner peace and found it through quieting my mind and meditating. I was able to see straight for the first time, like never before. So when times got tough, I knew what I had to do.

I turned inward, knowing that my vibration wasn't good where I was hurt or where I felt incomplete and started where I wanted to be. Keeping my eye on the prize was how I got through.

Issues were blaringly obvious. Being that what was happening seemed to be getting worse, I had to focus on what was going right somehow.

I can feel appreciation for what the contrast is showing me. And it is always showing you that everything is always working out for you.

Even as I look back now, I see that Bam and I's feet has never touched the ground. We always had a roof over our head, even if it wasn't our own. We've always had somewhere to sleep and eat. Bam always had a place to learn. Although it wasn't ideal, it was what we needed to get back on track.

I'm eternally grateful to my mother for that. No matter how messed up things became, I was grateful that Carrie did it in Florida. No hard feelings for how things turned out.

You want something in this life, a way to be made. Just allow the path. Easier said than done but definitely possible.

The funny thing about manifestations is that it's everything that unfolds in your life. Good and what is perceived as bad at the time but it all always works out.

"Everything always works out for me" one of my biggest mantras for my life.

Sometimes we manifest things that we don't want because we get what we think about whether we want it or not.

What I thought about and felt about permeated our lives and dictated our course until I finally started believing in myself and started to have faith in my ability to create the life we truly wanted. Now, we only think about what we want. And follow the impulses that bring us towards it.

It's like when you're driving in a car and you keep turning your head backwards, you start to swerve in the direction that your body's momentum goes in. I had to stop looking behind me; I was not going in that direction anymore.

All I wanted was to stop telling the stories about my son's father and how hard it has been. No. There is no Law of exertion, only the Law of Attraction. I had to stop attracting his micro aggressions by stopping my own.

All I know is that he loves our son. We must start from there. Every once in awhile, we will disagree on how to co-parent, but I promised myself that I will take the perceived control away because I CREATE MY OWN REALITY.

ME. MINE.

I resolved that I wouldn't tell this narrative of lack, deflecting where I am because it is the past. What I did from *now* would dictate the future that Bam and I will have.

I don't let 'now' circumstances overwhelm how I feel about my blessed existence. I know how it feels to allow my power to float away behind believing things that ended up hurting us. How could I show my son that we create our own reality?

Where is your power? Within YOU.
I have my mind. I remain consistently
confident in my creation. I am constantly
making new ideas and streams of income that
Bam and I will continue to roll over and over in
the future.

One day, I had looked on Facebook and in one
of the groups that I am in, a young woman
with the same aim was talking about a book
tour.

She was singing my song and definitely had in
common with me that it was time to share our
gifts with the world and help others find their
own gifts through entrepreneurship.

It was like a hug from the Universe. Everything
that I did up until now made sense. I really saw
clearly that all of the work that I was inspired
to do was now me getting ready to be ready to
be ready for this moment.

I immediately signed on.

At the time, I didn't know how I was going to be able to participate, but I knew that if I went for it and continued to get ready for it, that it would the how it would all come together for me. For me and Bam's future.

Now I was inspired to finish the books that my mind put on pause. I now found the words that coincided with who I am now and on track with who I wanted to become.

I learned to put a period on the end of the sentences and that I would definitely be telling more stories in the future but this was the chapter that I was done writing.

I was done losing and starting over. I was done with letting my life live me and I finally took control of the steering wheel that was my life and stopped floating aimlessly in the mediocrity that I was living.

I didn't want to just have potential, I wanted to win. Not just get to the destination, but also enjoy the ride that I was on.

Sometimes as we travel through life, there are rough times that we go through but you don't stop there, you keep going.
If you stop, you'll stay there. If I kept making left turns, then I'd continue going in circles.

I had to take control of my own reality. It was time to absolutely let go and allow the greatness that was always supposed to be our prosperity and abundance.

Sometimes we take the long road to manifestation because as imperfectly perfect humans, we believe there's always a struggle to get to what we want.

Why was I still choosing to struggle? Uhhhh! Why was I taking the long way to get to the *same* crossroads?

I learned:
- It's ok to leave people behind.
- It's ok to move forward and leave the past.
- The past is the past. Even now is the past.

- If doesn't apply to me anymore, let it fly past me.
- Remain aware of everything, but keep mind on my own business (vibration).
- Do what u can, leave behind what u cant...
- I had to decide that I was worth it. My dream, my mission was worth it. I needed me. That's all I needed to know.

I had to decide that I was worth it. My dreams, my mission was worth it.

I have a great multitude of friends and family. I love them so much for who they are and their gifts and generosity. But it wasn't my job to make them understand what my dreams were or to even sell it to them. I had to step away from it all to my own naked, scared dreamer of a woman that needed to drown out everyone else and fly solo like the Birdie I am.

And I know that they weren't happy with me. I did care but for my own vibrational purpose, I had to push myself to not care about opinions and my dream had to be bigger.

I just heard the words my son said, "Mommy, I trust you." The echo was all I needed on my hardest days. And even when my son was sad at our current circumstances I had to deflect his vibration and focus on what I wanted to feel. Like a good mother. Not the failure I felt like. I couldn't even think about my son's feelings, although I saw him everyday.

I woke up at 3:33 every morning, before Bam woke up. At 9, I'd wake him up for breakfast and to start schooling at 10.

I was laser focused on us. Building my son, building myself. Nothing else mattered.

This journey meant that I had to learn myself all over again, how my inner being really felt about me. Sitting alone, walking alone, being in the world without being of the world as I knew it before. I learned that all of my limits were self-made. We have all heard of people in this life have done a lot more with a lot less, with worst situations by comparison to overcome. But this was my own journey.

I also learned that I needed to finish what I started or it would haunt me, without letting it consume me. I am inspired constantly and when I don't go, I physically feel pain. My inner being simply won't allow it.

I believe that **everything** is always working out for me. For all of us. All of the contrast (things not wanted) helps us figure into what we do want, even if it was relief and release.

Ask, believe, receive... line up, allow.
The process is that simple, but we make it hard to live unscathed by the realities we create.

My life is a testimony to that fact.
Trauma is trauma, you can see thru it if you want to get out of it. We all feel pain. The thing about pain is that relief when the pain finally goes away. If pain is all that you're used to, it makes it easier to go back to the things that hurt you. Because it's what you're used to, that's your point of attraction until you change it.
Honesty. Brutal gut honesty. I felt like a bad mom, a horrible person, a bad friend. More

than anything I felt like the survivor of an apocalyptic event in an action packed movie. I survived *me*. I survived the past and I was still standing. I made it look crazy easy but I was a wreck. I needed safety. I had to retreat and regroup. I didn't have "permission" and a lot of people didn't understand but I had to decide that it was ok that no one understood.

I tuned into inner me.

It was how I achieved inner peace. Meditation. Fasting. Cleansing... I felt more clear.
I drank a lot of water and I slept more.

I started writing my goals. I wrote how I feel in regards to already having it. I started taking more walks. I wanted to feel good and it started with how I treated my body.

I conditioned my hair. I soaked myself in oils and massaged myself. In those moments I felt like I was orchestrating every minute and action and moment. I knew I had to follow my own advice. I looked in the mirror and loved myself again. I was not going to be ashamed of the fail. Because when we understand that it is always working out for us, was it even a fail?

I can laugh now when I think of it all. Every time a door didn't open, it was ME that the was missing key. I just went thru another door that had the room with the key for that previously locked door. My path literally lit up for me because I decided to walk in my own path. And I started to breathe…

We separate ourselves from the greatness that is us because even though we 'know' that we create our own reality, we forget that
WE CREATE OUR OWN REALITY!

I think that we let "What is" define the moments that we're currently submerged in that we forget to just let go and walk away.

When you put all of your attention in the rear view mirror and you're going forward, what happens. You hit the warning cones or the rumble strips or worse, eventually running off the road completely.

And if I didn't pay attention to my own vibration and how I truly felt about the parts of my life that needed my focus, I was just lying to myself.

So what was in my *"now"* What did I want?

What was my "Step 1, Ask"?

Wanting a home for my son and me.

I wanted to be proud of myself and my accomplishments, soar with what I had to offer.

I wanted my businesses to succeed.

I wanted to be a better co-parent.

I wanted to be prosperous.

My inner being felt that I already was, why didn't I live in harmony with who I really am?

So how do I get to where I wanted to be?

How does anybody?

The answer is NOW:

Be content *now*.

Be happy *now*.

Be satisfied *now*.

Love myself *now*.

Pay attention to how I feel *now*.

As I started that truth, I can't explain the weight that lifted off of me. My inner being version of now and the outside manifested "now" finally converged and made sense. I just had to tune into myself.

The how was provided for me for my book tour and what I needed for it all to happen on the grander scale than I could ever imagined.

I am so happy with my life now. What I've always wanted, I now have. The accountability that comes with the amount of clarity that I have now that the contrast that was temporary. Although falling backwards is repeatable, I could get back on track AT ANY TIME.

That's why this book was so important. This is the clarity of my example using The Laws, that attracted to me all of the circumstances that I didn't want because of my limiting beliefs and default living when I was supposed to be living so much better.

So how can I teach when words are not enough?

I have to not just thrive and survive but to be abundant and prosperous and that takes allowing the rewards of what I was getting ready to be ready for. I felt greatness so it all came to pass.

I also know that I'll never get my creation done and new contrasts and issues will present themselves but the difference between now and then is that how I feel won't dictate the outcome. My vibration will create my response. I'm so good with that.

Every problem has a solution. Was I going to keep praying and wanting or was I going to finally allow the answers to come to me? Meditation does that for me. When I have a problem, I can't give it my full attention and let it change my vibration. It will snowball and affect everything.
I just think of something that makes me feel better, even if it means to take a nap, using one of Jason Stephenson's guided meditations. It truly stops the flow of what I don't want to happen, if not slowing it down, making it easier to deal with.

I heard that anxiety is when worry borrows from a tomorrow that may never come. We create our own reality. The past is the past and reacting pushes it forward. We can't let what could happen steal the joys of today.

I maintain the vibration from the redirection and use what is flowing from that, to guide the future events. It's like that feeling from being caught in the current of raging waters, I always felt the rush of emotions and adrenaline from the pain, then take a walk, look at the sky, think of creation. See what I want, and think of where I want to see my next sunset.

Listening to the science behind the Law of Attraction, with Joe Dispenza and Bob Proctor, it's amazing to see how the mind works.
How we think, guides how we feel. How we feel, guides our physical response. Physical response guides how we react, reaction guides how we create.

That's why when things happen, it affects our lives so much.

There are countless cases of people who survive disease and horrific situations that changed simply because they changed their thinking. Not faking it, but through imagining the outcome that they want, bringing them into a new perspective how they create consciously.

When you've hit your own version of 'rock bottom', all you want is relief.

I saw myself as being abundant with all that I've ever wanted and deserved for myself. And I let it flow. The storm was over and I didn't need to examine the wreckage. I could walk past it because there was nothing that was worth my time or energy back there.

Bam and I manifested our new home that we always wanted. We used to walk and talk only about what that house would be. What it would look like, smell like. Going to open houses as if to look at our options. But we only felt like it when we actually felt like it.

There's a difference between going or doing something for the feeling rather than letting the feeling take us where we wanted to be.

We felt better. We treated that situation we were in as a nesting period. Some time to figure out what that version of being the best us truly were.

My businesses started to make so much money that I needed help to account for it for the first time ever.

I can truly say that I am blessed beyond all measure.

I love my life and I have built a legacy for my son that he's proud of and more than anything, if we don't want to do it, we don't force it.

If we want something, we draw it out. We intend it. We meditate on it and leave it alone. We only see that thing that we want and stay positive about that want. Nothing else. No more settling for a lesser feeling.

I just remember that feeling as we packed up my speaking materials from that day, after that speech. I heard Bam sigh. I looked at him. He smiled that smile that made my spirit swell.

"I'm so proud of you, Ma."

"Thanks Bam."

"So, what now?"

I smiled. "Now, we go home."

ACKNOWLEDGEMENTS

I'd like to thank myself for the understanding from believing the Law of Attraction for showing me my power. Good and not so good, I radiate and reflect the fact that I do and always will create my own reality.

Because of knowing my inner being and my own higher power, comforts me that everything is always working out for me.

I'd love to thank my Mom for allowing me to find myself on that couch with my Bam.

Bam, I'll never, ever be able to truly explain how grateful I am for your love, especially when things got worse before they got better.

The kindness and support of my family and friends that I manifested into my experience, And even those that my creation attracted that brought contrast into my existence.

There are so many teachers that have taught me about the importance of my own vibration and the life I want to create is within my own inner power. I do believe in God. I also believe in my own inner being that I have been gifted in believing. I create it based on the belief systems shown to me that I've had all along.

From this entire life experience words, thoughts and gifts that I receive gave me respite that I needed to sustain me. Through it, I helped me speak and live the language that I learned when no one else could understand me. It guided me to my understanding myself that I can teach through my clarity of the example set for me and through me for others to understand. I am truly appreciative of all of the lessons that living teaches and will continue to teach.

Thank you for letting me share my journey with you,
I love you. Birdie.

Breathe
THE PROCESSES:

The following processes and the access to listen to these breathing exercises can be found on BreatheByBirdie.com.

I'm hoping that these breathing exercises will help you as much as it has helped me in my life and through my respire practice.

Thanks for joining me as you Breathe with Birdie.

Please note: I am not a healthcare provider and you should get your doctor's permission before doing anything that could stress or strain you.

I only wish you the best.

Intro to Breathe...

Hey you,

Did you know that you create your current
reality?
The past is the past
And the present is just the residuals of the past.

Now is where you can turn it all around.
And we start by breathing.
Breathing in and out takes about 10 seconds.
10 seconds times 10 is a minute.
Changing your life, one minute at a time, you
can shift up.

The fact that you can breathe is great in itself.
In breathing, you can take back your power.

In breathing
I'm going to make it so that you can hear me
but you can breathe properly.

Breathing properly takes a little work, but when you get a hang of it, it will change everything!

Put your hand on your belly.
As you breathe in, you'll push your belly out.
As you breathe out, you'll pull your belly in to get the air out of your lungs like you're blowing into a balloon.

If you're just learning this method of breathing, it is very normal to get confused. Just breathe with the thought and focus back on your breathing. Counting on your fingers as you breathe in and out is another method. But don't dwell too much on the counting. Finding the breath that you're comfortable with is the most important thing.

Now, breathe in through your nose for 4 seconds.
(Remember, you're pushing your belly out)
Hold it for 2 seconds.
And breathe out through your mouth for 4 seconds.
(Deflating that belly, it's getting smaller)

Now, breathe in for 4 seconds.
Hold it for 2 seconds.
And breathe out for 4 seconds.

Now, breathe in for 4 seconds.
Hold it for 2 seconds.
And breathe out for 4 seconds.

Now, breathe in for 4 seconds.
Hold it for 2 seconds.
And breathe out for 4 seconds.

Now, breathe in for 4 seconds.
Hold it for 2 seconds.
And breathe out for 4 seconds.

Now, breathe in for 4 seconds.
Hold it for 2 seconds.
And breathe out for 4 seconds.

Now, breathe in for 4 seconds.
Hold it for 2 seconds.
And breathe out for 4 seconds.

Now, breathe in for 4 seconds.
Hold it for 2 seconds.

And breathe out for 4 seconds.

Now, breathe in for 4 seconds.
Hold it for 2 seconds.
And breathe out for 4 seconds.

Breathe in a Good Morning
Good Morning, You.

It's time to wake up.
It's a beautiful day because you have opened
your eyes and
You are here.
You want to have a great day.
For you to have a great day,
it's important to have the day that you really
want.
So let's set an intention.

Think of a car. You're behind the steering
wheel.
We want to have control over where we go and
how we get there.
Let's think of *where* you want to go.
You want to get there safely
So you *stay conscious* of *how* you drive on
that road.

We want to be the creators of our life,
not the reactors of our life.
So, let's be mindful of the energy we exude and
include in our vibration.

So after you've read these and gotten familiar on what to do,

Close your eyes and let's smile for 3 seconds.
Breathe in deeply through your nose, filling up your lungs.
Then breathe out, pushing all of the air back out.

Breathe again.

Smile. Breathe in deeply through your nose, filling your lungs.
Breathe out, pushing your breath all the way out.
Now, how do you want your day to go?

Now think of you outside, out and about Smiling to yourself because nothing, and I mean nothing, is going to change how great you feel inside.
Even when you are in a stressful situation that you cannot control, you will think to yourself, *"There's nothing I can do about this right now,*

So I'm going to focus on what I can control right now."
Even if it is to just breathe and smile to yourself.
Even if you want to just get through the day.

Think of what you really want to accomplish today.
Yes, there will be unexpected things that happen.

Remember, it is temporary and that **YOU** are the creator of your reaction.
Think about how you want to feel and have a great day.

You can continue for another minute or two.
I'm hoping that we smiled together with this great breathing exercise.

Thanks for joining me as you *Breathe with Birdie* Enjoy your day. And if all you did was breathe today, you did good.

Breathe to laugh: We're going to call this: Lions Breath-ish

I call it *Lion's Breath-ish* because we're not going into the full yoga pose call The Lion's Breath pose.
It's actually really great for raising your energy on a whole other level.

The truth is sometimes it isn't realistic at the time of stress to do some processes. We may not have the time or be in the place to actually get into full poses.

We're always on the go, but for this, we will find our cubicle, get comfy at our desk or take a quick break in the bathroom.

Disclaimer: We're going to get a little loud with our breathing.
So get ready for some attention or you can find a quiet place to be alone.

While sitting, put your hands on your knees, but relax.

Close your eyes, Breathe in through your nose deeply, and slowly pull your hands from your knees back to your thighs.

And when you breathe out, you're going to breathe out like you're fogging up a window or a mirror with the air going all the way out of your lungs, now pushing your hands from your thighs back to your knees.

Now you may get self-conscious about this next part but trust me, you will feel so much better afterwards.
So, as we breathe out, you will also be sticking your tongue all the way out and put your eyes towards the ceiling.

Yes, that's the breathe to laugh part. So smile.

Hands on your knees. Eyes closed. Breathe in, slowly slide your hands back to your thighs. Now breathe out, Eyes open to the ceiling, mouth wide, tongue out and hands sliding towards your knees. Hope you're fogging up that window.

Again…
Hands on your knees. Eyes closed. Breathe in, slowly slide your hands back to your thighs. Now breathe out, Eyes open to the ceiling, mouth wide, tongue out and hands sliding towards your knees. Hope you're fogging up that window.

Again…
Hands on your knees. Eyes closed. Breathe in, slowly slide your hands back to your thighs. Now breathe out, Eyes open to the ceiling, mouth wide, tongue out and hands sliding towards your knees. Hope you're fogging up that window.

You can continue for another minute or two. I'm hoping that we smiled together with this great breathing exercise.
Thanks for joining me as you **Breathe with Birdie.**
Enjoy your day. And if all you did was breathe today, you did good.

Breathe Out The Tension

Hey You,

You may be feeling highly tense right now.
But we are going to breathe out the tension.
It's different, but come along with me.
Find a nice quiet place.
Sit down, feet on the floor
Or if you're lying down this works too.
We're going to release the tension you're
feeling.

Now shrug your shoulders all the way up
Squeeze your eyes closed tight, wrinkling your
forehead
Close your mouth and clench your teeth
Ball up your fists and hug yourself tight
Scrunch your toes
And breathe in, tensing all of your muscles.

Now let it all go in a **whoooosh,** pushing **all** of
the air out of your lungs.

Relax your shoulders and drop your arms to
their sides
Un-ball your fists and toes
Relax your hands.
Smile. Open your eyes.

Breathe in, expanding your chest out
And breathe out, your chest should be deflating
from letting out all of the air.

Don't hold on to the stress. Release the tension.

Now breathe in,
And when you breathe out all of the air out of
your lungs.

Breathe To Change Your Vibe

Hey You,

Either someone upset you
Or a situation got you stressed out.
The good news is you don't have to stay there.
The great news is that you want to feel better.
The fact that you have the presence of mind
right now, in this moment is a step in the right
direction.
You care about how YOU feel in the moment.

You are thinking of what's best for you
Ultimately what's best for you is what's best
period.
So congratulations on taking care of yourself.
Let's breathe it out.

As we breathe in and out, listen to my words.

Breathe in
I'm so glad that I am taking care of myself

Breathe out.

I am so glad I'm creating my relief and release

Breathe in
I deserve to feel good.

Breathe out
I do feel better

Breathe in
I am easing my mind

Breathe out
It's getting better already

Breathe in
I'll be ready in a minute.

Breathe out
I really got this

You can stop here, find more great things to say as you continue to breathe in and out, or you can repeat from the beginning of the process.

Breathe into Gratefulness

By definition, being grateful
Means readiness to appreciate
No matter what we may be going through,
we have something to be grateful about.

Where you've been.
In heart and mind and body,
You aren't where you were.
You are present in this moment
You are able to breathe.
You are able to hear this.
You have your mind.
In that, we should be grateful.
Start there. Breathe into gratefulness.
Then you can expand your thought process.
You woke up today.
You have your mind to think.
You have the choice to love yourself.
You can choose to live.
And you can fill in the blanks with positive
thoughts thereafter.
And we can breathe together for one minute.

Breathe in through your nose
Deeply

The push all of the air from your lungs in
spurts 4 times as you push the air all the way
out
(Like: Blow, Blow, Blow, Blooooooooooooow)
all of the air out.

Repeat and Continue for another minute

Breathe Out The Bad Day In A Minute

Hey you.

I know that this is not a good time for you.
Good news is, you don't have to stay in this
moment.
It is temporary. We will not dwell on what
made it a bad moment.
Because if we stay there, it's only going to get
worse.

So let's breathe it out, so we can start to turn it
around. Let's do this like we did when we first
started our breathing together.

Now, we will breathe in for 4 seconds.
Hold it for 2 seconds.
And calmly breathe out for 4 seconds.

Now, we will breathe in for 4 seconds.
Hold it for 2 seconds.
And calmly breathe out for 4 seconds.

Now, we will breathe in for 4 seconds.
Hold it for 2 seconds.
And calmly breathe out for 4 seconds.

Now, we will breathe in for 4 seconds.
Hold it for 2 seconds.
And calmly breathe out for 4 seconds.

Now, we will breathe in for 4 seconds.
Hold it for 2 seconds.
And calmly breathe out for 4 seconds.

Now, we will breathe in for 4 seconds.
Hold it for 2 seconds.
And calmly breathe out for 4 seconds.

Now, we will breathe in for 4 seconds.
Hold it for 2 seconds.
And calmly breathe out for 4 seconds.

Now, we will breathe in for 4 seconds.
Hold it for 2 seconds.
And calmly breathe out for 4 seconds.

Now, we will breathe in for 4 seconds.
Hold it for 2 seconds.
And calmly breathe out for 4 seconds.

Now, we will breathe in for 4 seconds.
Hold it for 2 seconds.
And calmly breathe out for 4 seconds.

Breathe Out The Past

We will breathe all of the air out from your lungs, releasing the past.

Did you know that you create your own reality? I mean everything that you may think of, every minute of every day controls your day. What you dwell on, takes over your life. If you think about it, you know its true.
BREATHE IN
AND BREATHE OUT , RELEASE THE PAST

Fortunately, when you're having a bad moment in your day, and possibly in your life, realizing then remembering that it is only temporary may help you. You can turn it all around by simply not giving it anymore power.

I've learned how easy it is to make your day, week, month, even a year into a good or bad to describe it
 But I can also actually pinpoint just the same, at least one great time to define it.
I have that power.

I learned that you create the reality you live in. I decided to change how I was going to surmise my life.

There are things that I never talk about. Things you can't see when you look at me.
You are not alone in your pain.
When you think of the past, we can choose to stand in our strength and move forward.
You can be happy. And believe it or not, it's not hard at all.
As far what others have done to us, they cannot hurt us anymore, even if they're still in our physical experience, we won't let what they've done affect how we feel about ourselves.
Know that we are not alone in our pain. There are others like us.

(BREATHE IN DEEPLY
AND AS YOU BREATHE OUT,
PUSH THE AIR OUT IN A WHOOSH, RELEASING THE PAST)

I found strength in realizing 2 things. The past does not define me. And I do not, do not have to stay the past.

I got my power back slowly. One day at a time.

Hearing someone else's story never can take away from mine. SO we will not compare the pain.
 I am the one that defines it and gives it power. Or I can take away the power *from* that situation.
Either way, it's me. Me.
BREATHE IN
AND BREATHE OUT , RELEASE THE PAST

I remember being a victim.
Now I'm in the realization that I am a survivor.
Now I can think about a good time during my worst times.
I can close my eyes and remember when I smiled.
I can dig deeper and remember how good something tasted or remember what kind of sky it was on a good day.

When I was in my worst, I can remember a day when I had fun. How I felt. Not what happened before or even what happened afterwards. I can just stay in the moment.
Just how good I felt in that moment, on that day.
I can tell the stories where I laughed so hard to the point of tears.
Elaborating on the good times, I can fill that emptiness with laughter.

The before and the after of my happy event can't be what defined my life. I am happy with myself now and I can look at where I was and smile at who I was and be proud of who I am today.

Moving forward is not sweeping anything under the rug by any means.
I've realized that whatever you think of expands and can dominate entire pieces of my life. I know now that in that, the bad parts win.
We can't let the good in if all we think of is the hurt and pain.
So, I learned to breathe.

BREATHE IN
AND BREATHE OUT, RELEASE THE PAST

I learned that the hurt has no hold on my life.
I learned that the power is in me.
I have the control over my life.
Even my now is literally the past.

I can take a piece of my life and add it to the bricks of what built me to be the me I am now. I do not need to revisit the past to fix anything. I can change my life now.
I decide what I determine my life to be.
Nothing and no one else has that power.

I take my power back.
My life is my life.
I create my reality.
When I talk about what has happened in my past,
I can now look outside of myself and talk about it
without it dominating my spirit.
But I don't have to talk about it. I don't have to go
there. I have that choice too.
Going there and *not* going there takes nothing
from my experience.
My life is my life.

BREATHE IN
AND BREATHE OUT , RELEASE THE PAST

 I am powerful, I have value.
I love myself and I control my future.
I will not stand in my past. I will not stand in pain.
I will heal myself. The past does not define me. I
am in control now,

You hear that? You say the same and mean it.
Start this by taking a deep breath in and as we say
the first sentence, breathing out
and we can breathe together.

BREATHE IN
AND BREATHE OUT , RELEASE THE PAST

Now you can repeat after me as we release within our breathing:

Hurt has no hold on my life.
The power is in me.
I have the control over my life.
My life right now is the residuals of the past.
I will not stay in the past.
I can take pieces of my life
add it to the bricks of my past
that have built me to be the me that I am now.
I do not have to revisit the past.
That's not where my validity lies.
I decide what I determine my life to be.
Nothing and no one has that power over my life.
I take my power back.
My life is my life.
And I create my reality.
I have the choice.
I am powerful, I have value.
I love myself and I control my future.
I will not stand in my past.
I will not stand in pain. I will heal myself.

The past does not define me.
I am in control now.
No one can take that away from me now.
I love who I am.

My journey is one step at a time.
One day at a time.
I write the story.
For now
and for always.
I give myself permission for peace.
As we think of the peace we seek,
We will breathe for a minute. You may continue
after awhile
and you will as you find your own rhythm.

BREATHE IN DEEPLY
AND BREATHE ALL OF THE AIR FROM YOUR
LUNGS.

Breathe Into Rest

Hey you, it's time to rest.
So please get into a comfortable position.
A position that will enable you to take a short rest, or get your nights rest.
If you haven't set your alarm, please pause this and set your alarm.
Don't try this now if you are driving a car or doing anything else that requires concentration and/ or work.
It's time to rest.

To help this along, we will use the 4-7-8 method.
For this, we will
Breathe in for 4 seconds
Hold it for 7
And breathe out with all of the air in your lungs for 8 seconds

As you breathe in, you'll push your belly out.
As you breathe out, you'll pull your belly in to get the air out of your lungs like you're blowing into a balloon.

If you're learning this method of breathing, it is very normal to get confused. Just breathe the thought and focus back on your breathing.

When you begin to yawn
It is your breath, that is sending a message to your brain that your body is ready to slow down.
I want you to focus on your breath at all times. Your mind may drift off and they'll be a thought or 2 that pops into your head, please breathe into the thought then breathe out, letting it go and focus back on your breathing. Do that every time your mind drifts.
You will be fine.

Do this again and again.
You got this.
Nothing else matters right now. It's just you and your breath.

Breathe in for 4 seconds, push your belly out, feel the air filling up your lungs
Hold it for 7
Breathe out, pushing of your air out of your lungs, for 8 seconds, filling the balloon up

Keep focusing on your breathing as I fade into the background.
4 in
7 hold
8 all the way out

Thank you for Breathing with me. If all you did today was Breathe, you've done good.